CO-APO-291

NEVADA COUNTY COMMUNITY LIBRARY

NOV   2017

MATH YOU WILL ACTUALLY USE ™

USING MATH IN
SPORTS

CARLA MOONEY

rosen publishing's
rosen
central ®

NEW YORK

Published in 2018 by The Rosen Publishing Group, Inc.
29 East 21st Street, New York, NY 10010

Copyright © 2018 by The Rosen Publishing Group, Inc.

First Edition

All rights reserved. No part of this book may be reproduced in any form without permission in writing from the publisher, except by a reviewer.

Library of Congress Cataloging-in-Publication Data

Names: Mooney, Carla, 1970–.
Title: Using math in sports / Carla Mooney.
Description: New York : Rosen Central, [2018] | Series: Math you will actually use | Audience: Grades 5–8. | Includes bibliographical references and index.
Identifiers: ISBN 9781499438727 (pbk. book) | ISBN 9781499438741 (library bound book) | ISBN 9781499438734 (6 pack)
Subjects: LCSH: Sports—Mathematics—Juvenile literature. | Mathematics—Juvenile literature.
Classification: LCC GV706.8 M66 2018 | DDC 796.0727—dc23

Manufactured in China

METRIC CONVERSION CHART	
1 inch = 2.54 centimeters; 25.4 millimeters	1 cup = 250 milliliters
1 foot = 30.48 centimeters	1 ounce = 28 grams
1 yard = .914 meters	1 fluid ounce = 30 milliliters
1 square foot = .093 square meters	1 teaspoon = 5 milliliters
1 square mile = 2.59 square kilometers	1 tablespoon = 15 milliliters
1 ton = .907 metric tons	1 quart = .946 liters
1 pound = 454 grams	355 degrees Fahrenheit = 180 degrees Celsius
1 mile = 1.609 kilometers	

CONTENTS

INTRODUCTION

The Tigers high school basketball player dribbles the ball down the court. He comes to a quick stop before the foul line and darts to the right. The Rams player guarding him hesitates for a second, leaving him wide open. The player lifts the ball high above his head and launches it in an arc toward the basket. The ball swishes through the basket, and the score is tied.

The Rams coach immediately calls a timeout. There are only five seconds left in the game. The Rams have one last chance to score and win the game in regulation.

The coach scans the players as they huddle around him, and then he calls over his assistant. The assistant coach tracks the scoring for each player. He also tracks the number of shots and number of baskets made for each player in the game. He uses this data to calculate a field goal percentage for each player. The Rams senior center usually leads the team in scoring and may be a good choice to take the last shot. In this game, the center has 14 points for the team. The coach asks his assistant about another player, the sophomore forward. The forward has 10 points in the game. A junior forward has 8 points. Which player should the coach choose to take the last shot?

In this real-world situation, the coach can use math to determine which player has the best chance of making the last shot. The coach can calculate each player's field goal percentage. In

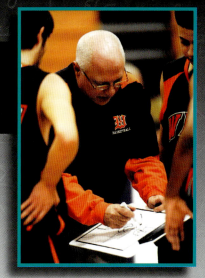

A basketball coach can use statistics to design the right play for his team.

basketball, field goal percentage is the ratio of field goals made to field goals attempted, multiplied by 100. It is abbreviated as FG%. Field goal percentage is calculated as follows: FG% = number of shots attempted ÷ number of shots made • 100.

The assistant shows the coach the following chart. The chart displays the data for each player.

Player	Total Points	# Attempts	# Baskets Made	FG%
Senior center	14	38	7	36.8%
Sophomore forward	10	25	5	40.0%
Junior forward	8	24	4	33.3%

Although the center has more points in the game, the sophomore forward has the highest field goal percentage. He has a greater chance of making the last shot. The coach quickly draws up a play to pass the ball to the sophomore. He will take the last shot to give his team the best chance to win.

CHAPTER 1

Using Arithmetic in Sports

From scorekeeping to converting measurements to calculating percentages, knowing arithmetic can help a person better understand sports in the real world. Fans and players alike benefit from being able to understand and analyze sports through numbers.

SCOREKEEPING

Many sports use math to calculate scores and determine who wins and loses. For example, scorekeeping uses addition. Some of the simplest scorekeeping addition occurs in sports like hockey, baseball, and soccer. In these sports, the team receives one point for every goal or run scored. Determining the score is simply adding one point at the time of each goal or run until the game is over.

Other sports, like football and basketball, add different numbers to determine the score. In basketball, the team scores two points for every regular basket made. If a player makes a basket outside the three-point line, the team scores three points. And foul shots each earn one point. In football, a team scores six points for every touchdown, followed by a try for two points during a two-point conversion, or one point for a kick. Three points can also be won for kicking a field goal. Using addition, you can determine the score for a team that scores three touchdowns, a field goal, and two successful tries for a kick: 6 + 6 + 6 + 3 + 1 + 1 = 23 points.

In gymnastics, a panel of judges uses addition and subtraction to score each gymnast's performance. The first panel starts with a score of zero and adds points when the gymnast performs required moves, difficult tricks, and connects one move to the next. The second panel of judges starts at 10.0 and subtracts points for execution and artistry. The gymnast's final score is determined by adding the two scores together.

Determining the score for the men's decathlon in the Olympics uses a lot of arithmetic. In the decathlon, athletes compete in 10 track and field events over two days. To count the

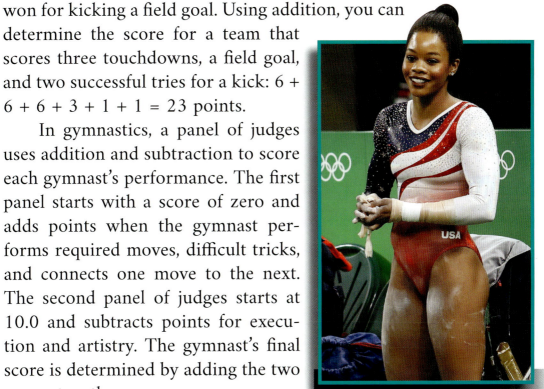

Gabby Douglas, an American Olympic gymnast, looks at the scoreboard during a meet to see what score she needs to take first place in the competition.

MATH ON THE JOB: ATHLETIC TRAINER

Athletic trainers use arithmetic every day in their jobs. John Anderson is an athletic trainer at Arizona State University. He helps evaluate, treat, and prevent injuries for athletes at the university. He uses math to calculate an athlete's target heart rate. He calculates target heart rate (THR): THR = 220 − the athlete's age. Then he works with the strength and conditioning coach to design a workout program for the athlete. The athlete wears a heart rate monitor during a workout. If the athlete wants to lose weight, they should work out at 50–70 percent of their target heart rate. If they want to improve their fitness level, they try to exercise at 70–90 percent of their target heart rate. The athletic trainer and coaches monitor the athlete to make sure he or she is working at the correct heart rate level.

results in each of these different events, decathlon scorekeepers use a points system. The athlete earns points based on a performance table for each event. The athlete's points are added together for each event. The decathlon winner is the person with the highest point totals after ten events.

AVERAGES AND PERCENTAGES

Averages and percentages are important statistics in many sports. Baseball regularly calculates batting averages and on-base percentages to rank players. In basketball, there are free throw percentages, three-point shooting percentages, and shooting percentages. These averages and percentages allow coaches and fans to compare individual players. They can also be used to compare entire teams.

For example, baseball teams use arithmetic to calculate each player's batting average with the equation: AVG = number of hits ÷ number at bats. Batting average (AVG) measures a player's batting ability. It compares the number of hits a player has to his number of times at bat. It does not matter if the hit is a single, double, or even a home run. Also, batting average does not include at bats where a player is walked or hit by a pitch.

In 2015, Jose Ramirez of Major League Baseball's Cleveland Indians had 176 hits during the regular season. He had 565 at bats. His batting average for the season was .312. A batting average over .300 is considered to be very good. The National League and American League award a batting title to the player in each league with the highest batting average.

CONVERTING NUMBERS

People also use arithmetic to convert numbers in sports. They convert numbers within

This baseball player is at bat. Whether or not he hits the ball, the outcome will go into his batting average.

a measuring system, such as converting from furlongs to yards. They also convert measurements between measuring systems, such as converting meters to yards.

In horse racing, sports announcers use math to understand and explain betting odds to listeners. Announcers and race fans convert betting odds into information they can understand. Take the Kentucky Derby as an example: it is one of the most famous horse races in the United States. Some people bet on which horse will win. In the Derby, a sports announcer may say that a horse is running at 5-to-2 odds. They can use arithmetic to figure out how much money a person betting on that horse will win. To figure out the answer, the announcer multiplies the first number by

At a racetrack, horses compete down the homestretch while fans cheer. Many of the fans may have placed bets on which horse will win.

TRY IT YOURSELF

Being able to convert numbers from one measuring system to another, or even within a system, is an important arithmetic-centered skill in sports. Runners often have to convert measurements from the imperial system's yards and miles to the metric system's meters and kilometers. Following are some practical situations in which conversions are necessary.

1a. A runner is training for a 10-mile race. One mile equals 1.609 kilometers. What is the distance of the race in kilometers?

1b. There are 1,000 meters in a kilometer. What is the distance of the race in meters?

two. Then the announcer divides the product by the second number. Finally, the announcer adds $2 to the result. For example, a person bets $2 on a horse with 5-to-2 odds. If the horse wins, the person will win $7. This is calculated as follows: payout on $2 bet = (5 • $2 ÷ 2) + $2 = $7.

YARDAGE TRACKING

In football, officials, coaches, players, announcers, and fans use arithmetic to keep track of yardage on the field. A football field measures 100 yards in length. Every five yards, white painted yard lines mark the field from sideline to sideline. The lines are numbered in intervals of 10. Also, every yard is marked with a white hash mark. The yard lines and hash marks tell players and fans how far a team must go to gain a first down.

To get a first down, the team on offense must advance the ball 10 yards. They have four attempts, called downs, to do it. If they achieve this, they get a first down, and this allows them four more

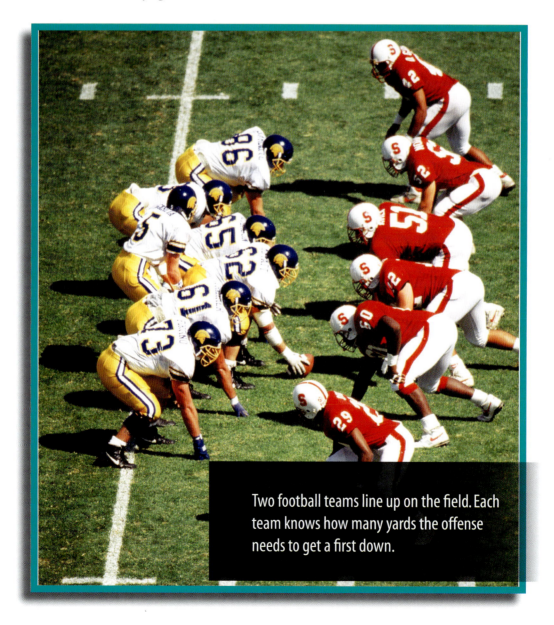

Two football teams line up on the field. Each team knows how many yards the offense needs to get a first down.

tries to go an additional 10 yards. If the team does not move at least 10 yards in four downs, the other team takes over the ball.

Arithmetic helps football players calculate how many yards they need to get a new first down. On the first play, the running back carries the ball for a three-yard gain. Subtraction tells fans that the team has seven yards to go $(10 - 3 = 7)$ to get a first down.

Also, announcers often talk about whether or not a team is in field goal range. Field goal range is the area of the field in which a team's kicker has a good chance of making a field goal. Arithmetic can determine where a kicker's field goal range is. For example, a high school kicker can kick a ball accurately from 40 yards. When the ball is on the 40-yard-line, the kick is longer than 40 yards. This occurs because the ball must travel through the goal post uprights. The uprights are at the back of the end zone, which is 10 yards deep. Therefore a ball kicked from the 40-yard line travels 50 yards $(40 + 10 = 50)$ to make it through the uprights. Also, the kicker does not kick exactly where the ball is marked on the field. Instead, he stands several yards back so that the linemen can protect him as he kicks. This can add 7 to 10 yards to a kick. When the ball is on the 40-yard-line, the kicker may stand at the 47-yard-line. This makes his kick 57 yards $(40 + 10 + 7 = 57)$. It is unlikely he will make the field goal.

The team can use subtraction to determine where the kicker is likely to make the field goal: 40-yard range − 10 yards end zone − 7 yards behind the line = 23-yard line. The kicker has the best chance of making the field goal if the team gets the ball to the 23-yard line or closer to the end zone.

CHAPTER 2

USING GEOMETRY AND TRIGONOMETRY IN SPORTS

A variety of sports use the basic principles of geometry and trigonometry. Understanding these branches of math can help athletes perform better, coaches create game plans, and architects design sporting fields and arenas.

BASIC GEOMETRY

Geometry is a branch of math that studies shapes, sizes, patterns, and positions. Sports fields and courts use geometry and shapes in their design. For example, a basketball court has many geometric shapes in its design. The court's perimeter is shaped like a rectangle. In the National Basketball Association (NBA), the court is 94 feet long and 50 feet wide. Smaller rectangles sit under each basket. These mark the free-throw lines, and markings around these rectangles designate bound-

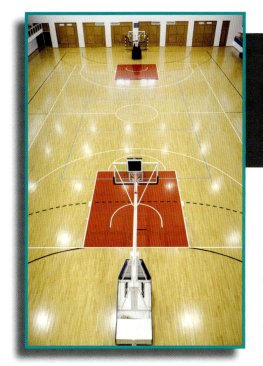

Lines on a basketball court show many geometric shapes that offer a reference for certain rules. For instance, the big white arc coming from the baseline marks the three-point line.

aries that players aren't allowed to cross until a free throw is complete. The free throw line is 15 feet from the hoop's backboard, so that impacts the size of the rectangle that contains it. The three-point line creates an arc at each end of the court. And the basketball hoop, the most important part of the court, sits 10 feet above the floor and has a diameter of 18 inches. Finally, the main piece of equipment in a game, the basketball, is a sphere with a diameter of about 9.55 inches. Knowing these measurements and geometric shapes can help a person approach practicing basketball at home.

ANGLES AND TRIGONOMETRY

Trigonometry is the branch of math that studies the relationships between the sides and angles of triangles. A ray is a line with a single endpoint that extends indefinitely in one direction, and an angle is the space between two intersecting rays or lines of determinate length, as measured in degrees. Combining rays and angles can create all kinds of shapes, many of which may be divided into triangles.

Angles are an important part of many sports. In basketball, players shoot the ball at an angle into the basket. Most basketball players know that if they shoot the ball straight at the hoop, it would probably just bounce off of it instead of going in. Instead, a basketball shot at an angle is more likely to go through the hoop because it makes the ball move in an arc that reaches into the bas-ket. Unless the shooter can reach higher than the rim, the ball rises up above the hoop's rim and then falls down into the basket.

Distance is important to consider, too. When a player shoots a free throw, he or she stands a specific distance from the hoop. The player shoots the ball at a narrower angle to get it through the hoop. When shooting closer to the basket, the player must shoot the ball at a wider angle . And, if a defender is trying to block the shot, the player must shoot the ball at an even wider angle to get it over the defender. Getting the ball's angle and arc correct for each distance keeps the ball on the right path toward the basket.

In soccer, understanding angles can help players score. When a player dribbles the ball close to the goal, he or she has to make a quick decision. Should the player pass the ball to a teammate, or should the player shoot? When a player kicks the ball toward the goal, he or she is trying to place the ball beyond the angle that defines the goalie's reach. Deciding how to make the shot, itself, also has an angle, and it can be represented by two lines that stretch from the player to each end of the goalkeeper's net. The width of the angle depends on where the player stands on the field. If a player determines that he or she can place the ball beyond the reach of the goalie, perhaps because he or she is straight in front of the goal or slightly to the side, he or she may decide to take the shot. If the player is standing far to the side of the goal, he or she may not have a good angle to shoot. The best option when there is no good shot is to pass to a teammate with a better angle.

Knowing angles is very important for goalkeepers in sports like hockey and soccer. In hockey, goalies learn how to cut down the angle of a shooter: they want to get in the best position to block as much of the net from the shooter's perspective. For example, a shooter directly in front of the net has the widest angle to shoot the puck. To cut off this angle, the goalie will skate out further from the net toward the shooter to block as much of the angle as possible.

In contrast, a shooter at the bottom of the faceoff circle has the narrowest angle. When the shooter has a narrower angle, the goalie plays deeper in the net. This allows him to have a shorter distance to cover to protect the net and prevent a goal.

This ice hockey goalie is mentally calculating which angle will offer the best option for guarding the net and preventing a shooter from scoring.

PYTHAGOREAN THEOREM AND THE ANGLE OF PURSUIT

In football, when an offensive player runs with the ball, a defender tries to tackle him. The defender wants to close the distance between himself and the ball-carrier as quickly as possible. He has to decide what direction and speed to run so that he can reach the ball carrier and tackle him.

Most defenders learn quickly that running straight across the field toward a running ball carrier's starting location will not work. The defender will get there too late. Instead, the defender should aim for a point on the field where the ball carrier is headed, not where he currently is. In the midst of a play, he has only a split second to estimate distance and velocity and decide what path to run. The path that the defender takes to intercept the ball carrier is called the angle of pursuit.

The defender's angle of pursuit is based on the Pythagorean theorem. The Pythagorean theorem relates the lengths of the sides of a right triangle, or a triangle with one 90-degree angle. In a right triangle, the two sides that extend from the 90-degree angle are called the legs (a, b), and the side that connects the legs is the hypotenuse (c). The Pythagorean theorem states that the square of the hypotenuse is equal to the sum of the squares of the triangle's two legs: $a^2 + b^2 = c^2$.

Here is an application of that concept:

If a receiver who just received a pass during third down is four yards away from the first down line and the defender is three yards away from the receiver, the defender will want to take down the

TRY IT YOURSELF

The quarterback in a football game has the ball at the line of scrimmage. His receiver also lines up at the line of scrimmage, 15 yards to the left of the quarterback. After the play begins, the receiver runs 20 yards straight toward the endzone.

2a. Draw a triangle that shows the points where the quarterback begins, the receiver's starting point, and the receiver's ending point. Label the quarterback's point as A, the receiver's starting point as B, and the receiver's ending point as C.

2b. Using the Pythagorean theorem, calculate how far the quarterback has to throw the ball to reach the receiver downfield.

receiver before the receiver scores the first down. Drawing lines to connect the three points—the receiver's position, the defender's position, and the intersection between the defender's path and the receiver's path—creates a triangle. Using the Pythagorean Theorem, the defender can estimate how far he needs to run to catch the receiver: $c^2 = 4^2 + 3^2 = 16 + 9 = 25$. To isolate c, find the square root of both sides: $\sqrt{c^2} = \sqrt{25}$, $c = 5$. Of course, to prevent the first down, the defender will have to be quick enough to keep the receiver from actually reaching the first down line.

Offensive players also use geometry and the Pythagorean theorem to help them run routes. Head coach Jason Garrett of the Dallas Cowboys gives geometry lessons to his wide receivers and quarterbacks. He explains that running in a straight line from the line of scrimmage to a point on the field takes a certain amount of

Jason Garrett (center), the head coach of the National Football League's Dallas Cowboys, believes that understanding geometry can help his players perform better on the football field.

time. But if the receiver lines up on the line of scrimmage 10 yards to the right or left, running to that same spot is longer because it is the hypotenuse of the right triangle. Understanding the difference, the receiver can adjust his stride to reach the spot as the quarterback throws the ball. Geometry can also help a quarterback better understand receiver routes and how they work together.

CHAPTER 3

Using Mathematical Physics in Sports

At its core, all sports depend on physics, a branch of science that studies matter and energy and how they interact with each other. Mathematical physics applies math to physics problems. The function of math and physics in sports is to explain how athletes, balls, and other objects move and interact.

MOTION AND FORCE

Motion is a key topic of physics with far-reaching applications. Everything in the universe moves. Some movement is very fast. Other movement is so slow that it is difficult to see.

The physics of motion starts with force. A force is a push or a pull that acts on an object to make it move, or to stop or change an object's motion. As it happens, forces are acting everywhere in the universe to cause objects to move at all times.

Sprinters rush forward as a race begins. Runners move their bodies in a particular way to go as fast as they can.

Scientists use a unit called a Newton (N) to measure forces. Force can be calculated as such: F (force) = M (object's mass) • A (acceleration that occurs). It demonstrates that how fast an object moves or accelerates depends on the size of the force and the object's mass.

Of course, in sports, forces affect the motion of athletes and their equipment. When someone hits a baseball, a measurable force acts on it. For example, if a baseball weighs .145 kilograms (kg), it's easy to figure out how big of a force would make it accelerate at 6.0 meters per second squared (m/s/s): F = 2.0kg • .145 m/s/s = .290 N. A force of .290 N will cause the ball to accelerate at 6.0 m/s/s. Knowing other factors, like the spin on the pitch, the angle of the swing, and air resistance would help determine exactly how far that .290 N would send the ball.

TRY IT YOURSELF

Here are some facts about a basketball: it is typically a spherical orange ball with black lines that allow for greater grip. Basketballs are usually filled with air so that they can bounce. And they are typically used on a hard surface to make bouncing them easier. In order to score points, a basketball player must shoot the ball into a hoop that must be larger than the ball—otherwise, the ball would just bounce off of it.

The basketball in question has a mass of .625 kg. When thrown at a hoop one particular time, it accelerates at a rate of 4.2 m/s/s.

3. What is the force on the ball?

NEWTON'S LAWS OF MOTION

Sir Isaac Newton was an English scientist that lived in the late 1600s. He studied forces and motion. Newton developed his three laws of motion to explain the physics of motion.

His first law states that an object at rest will stay at rest unless a force acts on it. In the same way, an object in motion will stay in motion unless a force acts to stop it. Newton's second law states that the acceleration of an object (its change in motion) depends on the size of the force and the mass of the object. His third law states that for every action there is an equal and opposite reaction. This means that if one object exerts a force on another object,

Sir Isaac Newton, an English scientist, studied motion and how forces affect motion. Today, his work remains an important part of our understanding of physics.

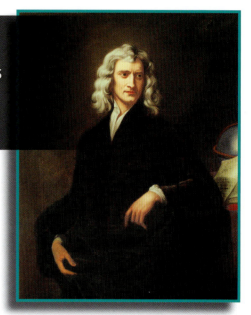

the second object will also exert an equal force back on the first object.

When a person hits or kicks a ball, they transfer kinetic energy from their body to the ball. An object that is moving is said to have kinetic energy. In baseball, the bat helps the player transfer kinetic energy to the ball more efficiently. Bats come in all shapes and sizes. They can be made from different woods, metals, or composites. The bat's design affects how efficiently it transfers kinetic energy and how the ball responds when hit. Balls also have different designs that affect how they react to being hit.

An elastic collision occurs when a hard bat hits a hard ball. In an elastic collision, all of the bat's kinetic energy before the collision transfers to the ball. Another example of an elastic collision occurs in pool when a hard ball hits another hard ball. When the first ball crashes into the second ball, it may stop suddenly. The first ball knocks the second ball away by transferring all of the kinetic energy that it carried.

But not all sports use hard balls and bats. Some sports use a softer object to hit the ball, such as a tennis racquet. Other sports use the athlete's arm or leg. In addition, some balls such as tennis or soccer balls are lighter and filled with air or other materials.

MATH ON THE JOB: SPORTS ENGINEER

Sports engineers use math and physics to solve various problems to do with sports. They design equipment, build facilities, and analyze athlete performance. Some sports engineers design cutting edge equipment. They create ergonomically designed shoes that help sprinters run their fastest and design tennis rackets that create the perfect spin on the ball. Some sports engineers work with athletes to help them interact with their equipment and improve their performance.

Sports engineers in the United Kingdom developed a new type of soccer goalkeeper glove. The new glove uses a special compound that is soft and flexible when moved slowly. When moved fast, such as when it is compressed by impact with the ball, the compound's molecules lock together. The material stiffens. This absorbs the impact and protects the goalie's hands while still allowing the glove to be flexible.

A sports engineer tests a prototype of a new piece of gym equipment with a volunteer to see if it works as it was designed to.

When a player kicks a soccer ball, an inelastic collision occurs. In an inelastic collision, not all of the kinetic energy is transferred. The ball deforms slightly during the collision with the player's foot, and this impact wastes some energy.

FRICTION

Another force that affects motion is friction. Friction is a force that opposes the motion of an object. Friction occurs when two objects come in contact with each other and move in opposite directions.

In sports, friction occurs between athletes, their equipment, and playing surfaces. There are several types of friction that affect the game of volleyball, a game where one team tries to hit the ball so that the opposing team cannot return it. Friction allows a player to hit, pass, and set the ball. Without friction, the ball would just slip through their arms or hands. When the ball flies in the air, friction between the ball and air can cause the ball to spin faster than it normally would. A ball with too much topspin is impossible to return.

In some cases, there is too much friction. When a player dives for the ball, friction between their skin and the court can cause a skin burn. Also, friction between a player's shoes and the court can cause the player to stop suddenly. This much friction can cause knee and ankle injuries.

DRAG

When a cyclist pedals in a race, the air resists his motion and slows him down. This air resistance is a type of friction called drag. Drag is a force that acts opposite to the motion of a moving object.

As the cyclists race around a track, a force called drag resists their forward motion. Leaning forward helps the air flow more smoothly over them, and reduces drag.

To reduce drag, cyclists wear teardrop-shaped helmets. They crouch over their bikes as they ride. This allows the air to flow more smoothly around them and reduce the drag force pushing against them.

Even swimmers experience drag forces in the pool as they move through the water. The friction of water pushes against them and slows them down. Also, it is easier to swim horizontally than vertically through water when moving from side to side because a vertical body going in that direction presents more surface area to collide with the water. Similarly, a vertical orientation is best for when moving straight up or down because orienting the body in an arrow-like fashion reduces the surface area for the water to drag against. Another measure swimmers can take is wearing special streamlined suits in the water that are meant to reduce drag and help swimmers move faster.

So bikers, swimmers, and other athletes must optimize their movements to account for forces that can negatively impact their performance.

CHAPTER 4

Using Statistics and Probability in Sports

S tatistics is a branch of math that deals with the collection, analysis, interpretation, and presentation of number data. In sports, statistics collects and analyzes data to give teams and athletes powerful insights and information. This branch of math relies on the assumption that past behavior is the best indicator of future behavior and relies on numbers to define those behaviors.

SPORTS ANALYTICS

People track wins and losses, hits and walks, shots and goals. In recent years, more teams are using sports analytics to help them make decisions. In 2011, the movie *Moneyball*, based on a 2003 book, introduced sports analytics to the general public. Actor Brad Pitt portrays the general manager of Major

League Baseball's Oakland Athletics, a man who believes that a player's on-base percentage is an important predictor of future performance. He uses that data to build a winning baseball team for less money.

Teams in all sports are aggressively using sports analytics to evaluate an athlete's performance. They rely on an analytics expert or an entire analytics department. In baseball, the analytics experts take data from scouting reports and general managers.

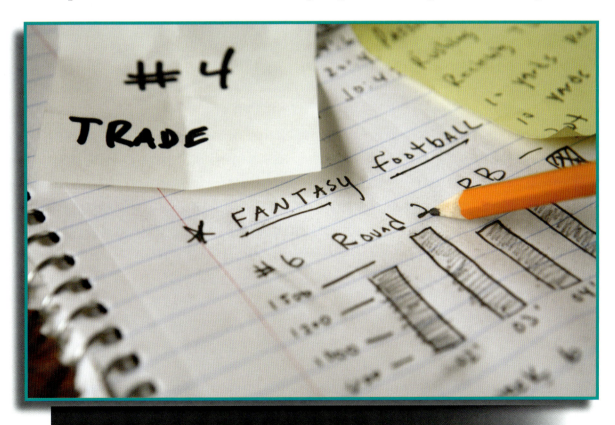

A person carefully studies a player's statistics from the previous season and statistics from the current season's projections. This evaluation helps to decide which running back to draft into a fantasy team.

These talented mathematicians analyze the numbers and create an overall profile of a player. They use this information to decide if a player is a good fit for the team. This information helps a team determine if they should draft a player, sign him as a free agent, or trade for him.

In basketball, NBA teams use analytics called "player tracking." This technology analyzes player movement to evaluate the efficiency of a team. The NBA team uses six cameras in their arena to track the movements of every player on the court and the basketball. The data is used to create statistics on speed, distance, player separation, and ball possession. With the data, teams can calculate how fast a player moves and how far he traveled during a game. Teams can also calculate how many times the player touched the ball, how many times he passed, how many rebounding opportunities he had, and many more statistics.

Even sports fans use analytics. Entire websites focus on research and analysis of sports statistics. They assess prior games, win-loss records, and opponent data. They use data to make predictions about future performance. Before the game is played, sports analytics can make a prediction of who will win based on numbers.

PROBABILITY

What is the chance that something will happen? Will it rain? Or will it be sunny? Will the Chicago Cubs finally win the World Series? Probability is a way of measuring in numbers how likely an event is to happen. The probability of an event is expressed as a percentage between zero and 100. Something that is impossible is

TRY IT YOURSELF

Statistics can compare teams and players. One measure of a running back in football is average yards per carry. Calculate this statistic as follows: average yards per carry = total yards gained ÷ number of carries.

4. Using the following table, determine which running back has the highest average yards per carry.

Player	Total Yards	Number of Carries
James Smith	551	200
Ron White	324	104
Leo McCoy	489	122

zero percent, while something that is certain is 100 percent. If the probability of rain is 75 percent, it might be a good idea to bring an umbrella.

In sports, there are many applications of probabilities. Before every football game, the official tosses a coin to determine which team will receive the ball at the start of the game. The probability that a team will receive the ball is: probability = number of events / number of outcomes. In a coin toss, there is one event: the toss. When the official tosses the coin, there are two possible outcomes. The coin will either land with the "heads" side up or the "tails" side up: probability = ½. Next, convert this fraction into a decimal, and

MATH ON THE JOB: SPORTS STATISTICIAN

Keith Goldner is a sports statistical analyst. He builds math models to evaluate players and teams in a variety of sports. He uses these models to project a player or team's performance. To begin, Goldner builds computer programs that find and extract data from official and fan websites. He uses several statistical models to analyze the data. The models also simulate how changes in the game might affect a team or player's chance of success. He can even tell a computer model to build the best roster around a specific player. Goldner also builds online tools that allow average fans to manipulate sports data to rank players or project the outcome of future games.

then the decimal into a percentage: ½ = .5; .5 • 100 = 50 percent. Therefore, if a team calls "heads," they have a 50 percent chance of the coin landing on "heads."

Coaches will use probabilities to help make decisions. For example, a football team has been successful on 2 two-point conversions out of 10 attempts. The probability of making the two-point conversion is 20 percent. The team's kicker has made 9 out of 10 extra-point kicks. He has a 90 percent probability of making an extra point. In a close game, the coach may decide to go for it.

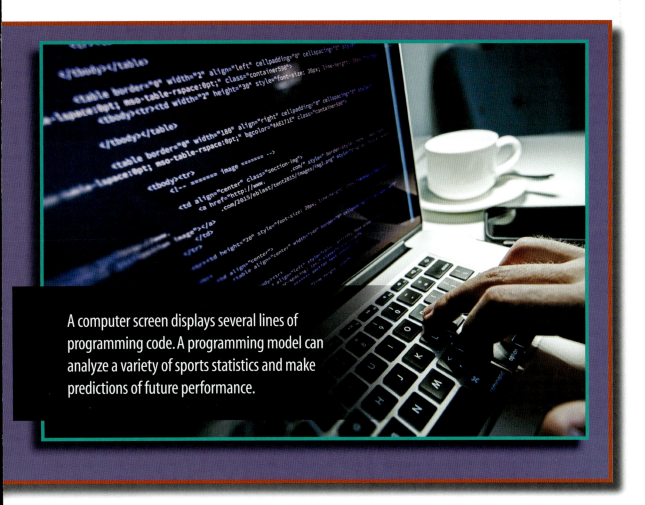

A computer screen displays several lines of programming code. A programming model can analyze a variety of sports statistics and make predictions of future performance.

MAKING PREDICTIONS

Statistics and probabilities are used to make predictions in sports. A prediction is a statement or forecast about an uncertain event. For an offense strategy in football, average passing yards, average running yards, and average points-per-game are some common statistical measures. Defenses also have statistics, such as average passing yards allowed, average running yards allowed, and average points-per-game allowed. To make a prediction about what will happen in the game, a person can compare statistics from the two teams. If team A has a high average of passing yards and team B has given up a lot of passing yards, it is reasonable to predict that team A's quarterback will throw a lot in the game. If team B's defense gives up an average of 10 points per game, it is reasonable to predict that team A will not score much in the game.

This soccer field has synthetic grass. The designers who created this field know that grass like this isn't as hard to maintain, and it offers a consistent terrain for the players from one game to the next.

RANKING TEAMS

Statistics are useful for ranking teams. Because of the sheer number of teams in the National Collegiate Athletic Association (NCAA), most college football teams do not play each other. Still, the College Football Playoff committee ranks the teams every week. The committee considers several factors in its weekly ranking. One important factor is a team's strength of schedule. Strength of schedule is a statistic that measures the difficulty of a team's opponents as compared to other teams. Strength of schedule can be calculated in many ways. One method is the following: strength of schedule (SOS) = (2 [opponents' winning percentage] + [Opponents' opponents' winning percentage]) ÷ 3. So if a team's opponents have a cumulative record of 55 wins and 33 losses, they have a winning percentage of 0.625 (55 wins ÷ 88 total games). The team's opponents' opponents have a winning percentage of 0.547. The team's SOS is: $(2[0.625] + [0.547]) ÷ 3 = (1.25 + 0.547) ÷ 3 = 1.797 ÷ 3 = 0.599$.

Various schools of math can help players improve their performance. It gives coaches an edge in preparing for competition, and helps people to design cutting-edge sports stadiums, surfaces, and equipment. The most sophisticated games emerge from developments in math, and will do so for years to come. The only way to take advantage of these continuing developments is to learn all that's available to about math in sports, and apply it to the performance of the game of choice.

ANSWERS

Answer 1a. The race is 16.09 kilometers: 10 miles (mi) = 10 mi • 1.609 kilometers (km) ÷ 1 mi = 16.09 km.

Answer 1b. The race is 16,090 meters: 16.09 km = 16.09 km • 1,000 meters (m) ÷ 1 km = 16,090 m.

Answer 2a. Label the sides of the triangle that meet at the 90 degree angle as 15 yards for the base and 20 yards for the height. The height should extend from the left side of the base since the receiver, who will run 20 yards, is to the left of the quarterback. Connect this line to complete the triangle.

Answer 2b. The following equation demonstrates that the quarterback must throw the ball 25 yards: $c^2 = 15^2 + 20^2 = 225 + 400 = 625$; $\sqrt{c^2} = \sqrt{625}$; $c = 25$.

Answer 3. Apply the equation force = mass • acceleration: .625 kg • 4.2 m/s/s = 2.625 N.

Answer 4. Each running back's yards per carry is as follows: James Smith's average yards per carry = 551 ÷ 200 = 2.755. Ron White's average yards per carry = 324 ÷ 104 = 3.115. Leo McCoy's average yards per carry = 489 ÷ 122 = 4.008. Leo McCoy has the greatest number of yards per carry.

GLOSSARY

ACCELERATION The rate of speed of an object.

ANGLE The distance between two intersecting lines or rays in degrees.

ARITHMETIC The branch of math dealing with numbers and the four basic processes of addition, subtraction, multiplication, and division.

AVERAGE The number found by adding a group of numbers together and then dividing the sum by the number of figures added.

DIAMETER The length of a straight line through the center of a circle.

DRAG A force that pushes against an object and opposes movement.

FORCE A push or a pull on an object.

FRICTION A force that occurs when two objects contact each other and move in opposite directions.

FURLONG An eighth of a mile, a measurement often used in horse racing.

GEOMETRY A branch of math that deals with shapes, sizes, patterns, and positions.

HYPOTENUSE The side of a right triangle that is opposite the 90 degree right angle.

KINETIC ENERGY The energy of an object in motion.

MASS The amount of physical matter an object contains.

NEWTON The unit for measuring force.

PERCENTAGE A fraction of something, usually written as a number out of 100.

PROBABILITY The chance that an event will happen.

PYTHAGOREAN THEOREM The relationship between the three sides of a right triangle: a^2 (length of the smaller side squared) + b^2 (length of the other smaller side squared) = c^2 (length of the hypotenuse squared).

RATIO A comparison of two numbers that preserves proportion.

RAY A line with one endpoint that extends indefinitely in the other direction.

RIGHT TRIANGLE A triangle with one 90 degree angle.

STATISTICS A branch of math that deals with analyzing and interpreting data and numbers.

TRIGONOMETRY A branch of math that deals with the lengths and angles of triangles.

FOR MORE INFORMATION

American Statistical Association
732 North Washington Street
Alexandria, VA 22314
(703) 684-1221
Website: http://www.amstat.org
This association provides many educational resources, including information about student competitions and student chapters of the organization.

Canadian Mathematical Society
209-1725 St. Laurent Blvd.
Ottawa, ON K1G 3V4
Canada
(613) 733-2662
Website: https://cms.math.ca
This society promotes the advancement, discovery, learning, and application of mathematics in Canada.

Major League Baseball
245 Park Avenue, 31st Floor
New York, NY 10167
(212) 931-7800
Website: http://mlb.mlb.com/home
Major League Baseball's website offers data on players and teams that can be used for math calculations and statistical analysis.

Mathematical Association of America
1529 18th Street NW
Washington D.C. 20036
(202) 387-5200
Website: http://www.maa.org
This association is the largest mathematical society in the world. Its website provides information for students about academic programs, student memberships, conferences, and other resources.

National Council of Youth Sports
7185 S.E. Seagate Lane
Stuart, FL 34997
(772) 781-1452
Website: http://www.ncys.org
This council supports the youth sports industry by offering background screenings, policy advocacy, and training to enhance the experience of youth sports participation.

National Football League
345 Park Avenue
New York, NY 10154
Website: http://www.nfl.com
The National Football League's website has an entire page on player and team statistics for current and past seasons.

Statistical Society of Canada
219-1725 St. Laurent Blvd.
Ottawa ON K1G 3V4
Canada
+1 (613) 733-2662 x 755
Website: http://www.ssc.ca/en
This society encourages the development and use of statistics
   and probability. It has information about Census at School,
   an international classroom project in which students train
   in statistical reasoning, using data collected about them-
   selves and about students from around the world.

WEBSITES

Because of the changing nature of internet links, Rosen Publishing has developed an online list of websites related to the
subject of this book. This site is updated regularly. Please use
this link to access this list:

http://www.rosenlinks.com/MYWAU/sports

FOR FURTHER READING

Belsky, Gary, Neil Fine. *On the Origins of Sports: The Early History and Original Rules of Everybody's Favorite Games*. New York, NY: Workman Publishing, 2016.

Doeden, Matt. *Fantasy Basketball Math: Using Stats to Score Big in Your League* (Fantasy Sports Math). North Mankato, MN: Capstone Press, 2016.

Frederick, Shane. *Football Stats and the Stories Behind Them: What Every Fan Needs to Know* (Sports Stats and Stories). Mankato, MN: Capstone, 2016.

Graubart, Norman. *The Science of Baseball* (Sports Science). New York, NY: Powerkids Press, 2015.

Graubart, Norman. *The Science of Basketball* (Sports Science). New York, NY: Powerkids Press, 2015.

Heos, Bridget. *Brain Quest Workbook: Grade 5*. Workbook edition. New York City, NY: Workman Publishing Company, 2015.

Kawa, Katie. *The Science of Gymnastics* (Sports Science). New York, NY: Powerkids Press, 2015.

Kleist, Nick. *Super Sports Numbers: Understand Place Value* (Rosen Math Readers). New York, NY: Rosen Classroom, 2014.

Koll, Hilary. *A Math Journey Through Extreme Sports* (Go Figure!). St. Catharines, ON: Crabtree Publishing, 2016.

Kortemeier, Tom. *Pro Baseball by the Numbers* (Pro Sports by the Numbers). Mankato, MN: Capstone, 2016.

Kortemeier, Tom. *Pro Basketball by the Numbers* (Pro Sports by the Numbers). Mankato, MN: Capstone, 2016.

Murphy, Cait. *A History of American Sports in 100 Objects*. New York, NY: Basic Books, 2016.

National Geographic Kids. *Weird but True Sports: 300 Wacky Facts About Awesome Athletics*. Des Moines, IA: National Geographic Children's Books, 2016.

Peterson, Altair, and Chris Pearce. *Everything You Need to Ace Math in One Big Fat Notebook: The Complete Middle School Study Guide* (Big Fat Notebooks). New York City, NY: Workman Publishing Company, 2016.

Rutledge, Johnny. *Grant's Sports Adventures: Math and Football*. Herndon, VA: Mascot Books, 2016.

BIBLIOGRAPHY

Austin, Clare. "Goalies 101: Cutting Down The Angle." *InGoal Magazine*, March 11, 2016. http://ingoalmag.com/features /goalies-101-cutting-angle/.

Barrow, John. "Decathlon: The Art of Scoring Points," University of Cambridge, retrieved October 28, 2016. http://sport .maths.org/content/decathlon-art-scoring-points-0.

Bow, Patricia. *Tennis Science*. New York, NY: Crabtree, 2009.

Clark, Kevin. "Cowboys are Hoping Practice + Math = Play-offs." *Wall Street Journal*, August 12, 2013. http://www.wsj .com/articles/SB10001424127887324085304579008754283 995522.

Coolman, Robert. "What Is Trigonometry?" LiveScience, May 30, 2015. http://www.livescience.com/51026-what-is -trigonometry.html.

Davoren, Julie. "Careers That Combine Math & Sports." *Houston Chronicle*, retrieved October 28, 2016. http://work.chron .com/careers-combine-math-sports-24662.html.

McDonnell, Steve. "How Sports Announcers Use Math." *Houston Chronicle*, retrieved October 28, 2016. http://work.chron .com/sports-announcers-use-math-4127.html.

Parrish, Rogue. "Which Angles Are Better for Soccer Scoring?" Livestrong.com, January 9, 2016. http://www.livestrong .com/article/489154 which-angles-are-better-for-soccer -scoring/.

PBS LearningMedia. "Real Life Math." Arizona PBS video, 6:59. Retrieved October 28, 2016. http://ny.pbslearningmedia .org/resource/mkaet.math.rp.athletictrainer/real-life -math-athletic-trainer/.

Peterson, Dan. "Coaching the Angle of Pursuit with Geometry." USA Football, August 5, 2013. http://usafootball.com/blog /fundamentals-and-performance/coaching-angle-pursuit -geometry.

Sawchick, Travis. "Clemson assistant Steele: Football 'all about angles.'" *Post and Courier*, October 26, 2011. http:// www.postandcourier.com/sports/clemson-assistant -steele-football-all-about-angles/article_bdbafc4f-f562 -525e-94b6-f68ac25da67c.html.

Steinberg, Leigh. "Changing the Game: The Rise of Sports Analytics." *Forbes*, August 18, 2015. http://www.forbes.com /sites/leighsteinberg/2015/08/18/changing-the-game-the -rise-of-sports-analytics/#57944ea031b2.

University of Cambridge. "Maths and Sport: Millennium Mathematics Project." Retrieved October 28, 2016. http://sport .maths.org/content/.

Vilorio, Dennis. "Interview with a Sports statistical analyst: Kevin Goldner Chicago, Illinois." Bureau of Labor Statistics, September 2015. http://www.bls.gov/careeroutlook/2015 /interview/sports-statistical-analyst.htm.

Woodford, Chris. "The Science of Sport." ExplainThatStuff.com, March 9,2016. http://www.explainthatstuff.com/science -of-sport.html

INDEX

ABOUT THE AUTHOR

Carla Mooney is a graduate of the University of Pennsylvania. Before becoming an author, she spent several years working with numbers as an accountant. Today, she writes for young people and is the author of many books for young adults and children. Mooney is a lifelong sports fan and enjoys learning how math and science impact her favorite sports and athletes.

PHOTO CREDITS

Cover, p. 1 Chris Ryan/Caiaimage/Getty Images; p. 5 Karl Gehring/Denver Post /Getty Images; p. 7 Tim Clayton-Corbis/Corbis Sport/Getty Images; p. 9 Cynthia Farmer/Shutterstock.com; p. 10 Cheryl Ann Quigley/Shutterstock.com; p. 12 David Madison/The Image Bank/Getty Images; p. 15 Muratsenel/iStock /Thinkstock; p. 17 Isantilli/Shutterstock.com; p. 20 Mitchell Leff/Getty Images; p. 22 Moodboard/Thinkstock; p. 24 Imagno/Hulton Archive/Getty Images; p. 25 PMN Photo/Shutterstock.com; p. 27 John P Kelly/The Image Bank/Getty Images; p. 29 © iStockphoto.com/spxChrome; p. 33 Welcomia/iStock/Thinkstock; p. 34 ©iStock/Sophie Caron; interior pages background Marina Sun/Shutterstock.com.

Design: Brian Garvey; Layout Design: Greg Tucker; Editor: Bernadette Davis; Photo Researcher: Sherri Jackson